YOUNG WOMEN
AND THE HPV VACCINE

JENNIFER BRINGLE

rosen publishing's
rosen
central®

NEW YORK

Published in 2012 by The Rosen Publishing Group, Inc.
29 East 21st Street, New York, NY 10010

Copyright © 2012 by The Rosen Publishing Group, Inc.

First Edition

Library of Congress Cataloging-in-Publication Data

Bringle, Jennifer.
Young women and the HPV vaccine / Jennifer Bringle. — 1st ed.
     p. cm. — (Girls' health)
Includes bibliographical references and index.
ISBN 978-1-4488-4575-0 (lib. bdg.)
1. Papillomavirus vaccines — Juvenile literature. 2. Papillomaviruses — Juvenile litera-
ture. 3. Teenage girls — Health and hygiene — Juvenile literature. I. Title.
QR189.5.P36B75 2012
616.9'11 — dc22

                                                            2011008645

Manufactured in the United States of America

CPSIA Compliance Information: Batch #S11YA: For further information, contact Rosen Publishing, New York, New York, at 1-800-237-9932.

CONTENTS

INTRODUCTION

Over the past few years, you have probably seen commercials on television for a vaccine that helps reduce the risk of cervical cancer in young women. Commonly known by the brand names Gardasil and Cervarix, this vaccine helps protect young women against the human papillomavirus (HPV), which is associated with a type of sexually transmitted infection (STI). Various subtypes (strains) of HPV cause a very common STI known as genital warts. Because HPV infection can have relatively few signs and symptoms at first, many don't even know that they have the virus. What makes HPV so dangerous for young women is that other subtypes of the virus can cause cancerous changes in the cells of the cervix, which is a round area located at the bottom of a woman's uterus that has an opening. Cervical cancer is one of the most common and dangerous forms of cancer in women. Because the HPV vaccine helps prevent infection, it also helps guard young women against the risk of developing cervical cancer.

Currently, the HPV vaccine is recommended for girls and women ages eleven to twenty-six. Because of this, many young women must get their parents' permission in order to get the vaccine. For some, that may be a scary prospect, since it means that they might have to talk to their parents about being or eventually becoming sexually active. The important thing for young women to remember is that parents or other trusted adults are a good source of information and support, and they are the right people to turn to when you are thinking about becoming sexually active. Because reducing the risk of cervical cancer is such an important thing, getting the vaccine is a worthwhile medical procedure.

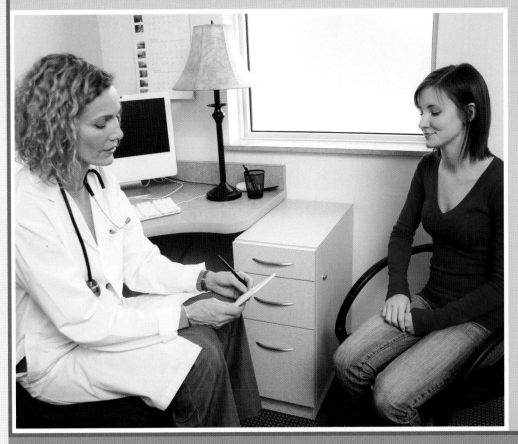

Young women who are interested in the HPV vaccine should talk to their parents and a trusted doctor or health care provider. A doctor can answer questions about the vaccine.

Before considering the HPV vaccine, it is important to know about the medication and how it works. It is also essential to know about HPV itself—what it is, how it is transmitted, its symptoms, and the effects of HPV disease. The only way you can stay safe and avoid STIs is to be educated about diseases and know how to avoid them.

CHAPTER one

WHAT IS HPV?

Genital human papillomavirus, most commonly known as HPV, is the most common STI. There are more than forty types of HPV that can cause anogenital (involving the anus and/or genitalia) infections in both men and women. Most types of HPV cause infections in the genital area, but some types can also infect the mouth and throat. In females, infection with certain types of HPV can increase the risk of getting cervical cancer. Unfortunately, many people who are infected with HPV do not even know that they have the disease. This is one of the reasons why it is such a dangerous STI.

HOW HPV IS TRANSMITTED

HPV is a viral infection spread between people through contact during oral, anal, and genital sex. There are more than one hundred types of HPV. Some types cause harmless conditions such as common plantar (relating to or occurring on the undersurface of the foot) and hand warts. More than forty types of HPV can infect the anogenital area—the vulva, vagina, cervix, rectum, anus, penis, or scrotum. HPV is a very common infection. It is estimated that about half of all sexually active men and about 75 percent of all sexually active women have had the infection at some point in their lives. According to the Centers for Disease Control and Prevention

Sexually active couples should always use condoms to prevent the transmission of diseases like HPV. The HPV vaccine can also help prevent the spread of the disease.

(CDC), approximately twenty million Americans are currently infected with HPV. Another six million people become newly infected each year.

HPV is passed between people through close contact and the exchange of body fluids, most often during genital or anal sex. It can also be transmitted through oral sex or genital-to-genital contact. The disease can be passed between both opposite-sex and same-sex couples, even if the infected partner has no signs or symptoms.

Most people infected with HPV do not realize that they have the disease. As a result, they do not know that they are passing the disease along to others during sexual contact. A person can have the disease even if years have passed since contact with an infected person. It is also possible to get more than one type of HPV. Very rarely, if a pregnant woman has HPV, she can pass the infection along to her child during birth. If this happens, the child can get recurrent respiratory papillomatosis. This rare disease can cause warts inside the throat, which obstruct breathing.

HPV SYMPTOMS AND EFFECTS

HPV often goes undiagnosed because there are no symptoms most of the time. In most cases, the body's immune system can clear up the infection within two years. This makes HPV especially easy to spread, because infected partners have no idea that they are passing it on to others during the time of infection.

In some cases, though, HPV does cause noticeable symptoms. The most common of these is genital warts, caused only by certain strains. According to the CDC, about 1 percent of sexually active adults in the United States have genital warts at any one time. These warts are most often small bumps or groups of bumps on the genital area. These bumps can vary in appearance—they can be small or large, raised or flat, or even shaped like a cauliflower. Warts can show up within weeks or months after sexual contact with an infected person, even if that person does not have visible symptoms. If left untreated, genital warts can go

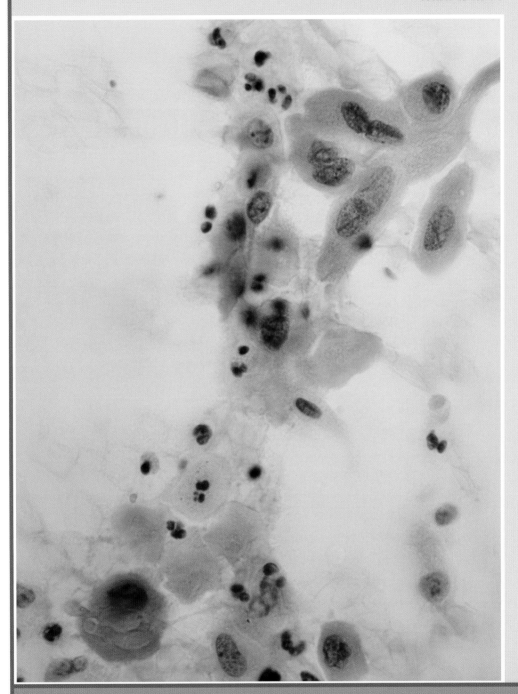

Precancerous cells detected during a Pap smear can indicate
a high risk for developing cervical cancer. These cells are often
formed as a result of an HPV infection.

away on their own. They can also remain unchanged or even increase in size or number—it varies with each individual case. It is important to know that the warts are caused by different types of HPV and will not turn into cancer.

HPV-associated genital warts are treated in a number of ways, depending on the size and number of the warts. One form of treatment is the use of topical cream or solution, which is applied directly onto the wart by the patient. This treatment can take up to sixteen weeks to clear up the warts. Another treatment is removal by liquid nitrogen. A health care professional will apply liquid nitrogen to the wart. The liquid nitrogen then "freezes" the wart, making it stiff and eventually causing it to fall off. Health care professionals sometimes remove warts surgically—either using tools to cut them out or lasers to burn them off. The primary goal of treating visible genital warts is the removal of the warts. In the majority of patients, treatment can induce wart-free periods. Unfortunately, while these treatments can reduce the frequency or numbers of genital warts, they do not necessarily eliminate the HPV infection itself.

Certain strains of HPV are far more dangerous. These types can lead to cervical cancer in women. Other kinds of HPV can also lead to other less common, but still dangerous, cancers, including those of the vulva, vagina, penis, anus, and head and neck (tongue, tonsils, and throat). The types of HPV that cause genital warts are not the same strains that cause cancer. There is no way of knowing which people who contract HPV will go on to get warts, cancer, or other complications.

Diagnosis of HPV often happens during regular gynecological examinations. Most women diagnosed with the disease find out as a result of having an abnormal Pap test result. A Pap test or Pap smear is part of a regular gynecological exam, where a doctor swabs a small number of cells from a woman's cervix to be tested for abnormalities under the microscope and in the laboratory. Abnormal cells caused by HPV can be seen through this test.

Another method of diagnosing HPV is through the HPV test for women. This method is less commonly used and usually only in specific situations, such as:

- When Pap tests show the presence of abnormal cells
- When Pap test results are not clear

Sometimes Pap smears aren't clear, or indicate the presence of abnormal cells. In this case, a health care provider may request that the patient take an HPV test to rule out the disease.

- For women over the age of thirty when they have a Pap test
- If a woman requests the test

Doctors do not usually recommend direct testing for HPV, because the disease is very common and usually goes away on its own without causing any additional health problems.

It can be very scary to realize that you may have contracted an STI. You may be worried about how you got the disease, how you will tell your partner that you are infected, or how you will get treatment for the infection. You may feel very alone or like you've done something wrong. These feelings are very natural. You may also be very afraid to go to your parents or guardian for help, if you are still living under their care. Talking to a parent or trusted adult, such as a doctor or teacher, is a good idea if you think you may have contracted HPV or any STI. If you have been infected with a disease, it is very important to be diagnosed and receive treatment as soon as possible. Even if you don't think you have the disease, it is important to talk to an adult if you are sexually active so that you can be fully aware of all the risks, including HPV. Becoming sexually active is a big step, and you should only do it when you are completely ready and have all the information you need to stay safe and healthy.

10 GREAT

QUESTIONS TO ASK YOUR DOCTOR

1 How can I avoid getting an HPV infection?

2 Do condoms prevent the transmission of HPV?

3 How will I know if the HPV vaccine is right for me?

4 If I find out I have HPV, how do I tell my partner?

5 How do I know if a bump is a genital wart, or something less serious, such as an ingrown hair?

6 What should I do if I see warts on my genitals?

7 How can HPV lead to cervical cancer?

8 Where can I get the HPV vaccine? Do I need my parents' permission to get the vaccine?

9 If I can't afford the vaccine, are there ways to get help paying for it?

10 How do I talk to my parents about HPV and getting the vaccine?

CHAPTER two

HPV AND CANCER

Cervical cancer is one of the most dangerous diseases a woman can get. It is one of the deadliest forms of cancer, because it can be difficult to diagnose and is often very advanced when it is diagnosed. Many women who develop cervical cancer do not know that they have it because its symptoms take a while to show up.

THE LINK BETWEEN HPV AND CERVICAL CANCER

High-risk HPV infections can lead to something far more serious than genital warts—they can cause cancer. High-risk HPV infections are linked to anal, penile, vulvar, vaginal, and, most commonly, cervical cancer. In fact, almost all cervical cancers are the result of HPV infections. According to the National Cancer Institute (NCI), it was estimated in 2007 that eleven thousand women in the United States would be diagnosed with this type of cancer and nearly four thousand would die from it. Cervical cancer strikes nearly half a million women each year worldwide and claims a quarter of a million lives.

When a woman gets a high-risk strain of HPV, the virus can cause certain cells to become abnormal. Both high-risk and low-risk

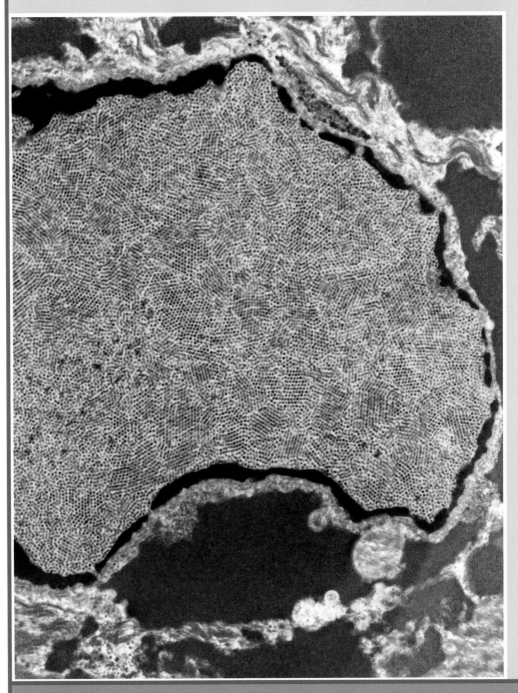

Some strains of HPV, such as this one embedded in the middle of a normal cell, can cause genital warts in infected persons. These warts are not as common as many think.

types of HPV can cause the growth of abnormal cells, but only the high-risk types lead to cervical cancer. More than a dozen types of high-risk HPV are linked to cancer, and these types produce growths on the cervix that are usually flat and nearly invisible (in contrast to the external warts caused by low-risk types).

However, abnormal cells do not always become cervical cancer. Even among the women who do develop abnormal cell changes with high-risk types of HPV, only a small percentage would develop cervical cancer if the abnormal cells were not removed. Generally, the rate of change of abnormal cells determines the risk of cancer. Thus, the more severe the abnormal cell change, the greater the risk of cancer. Studies suggest that whether a woman develops cervical cancer depends on a variety of factors acting together with high-risk HPV infections. Several factors can increase the risk of cervical cancer in women with HPV infections, including smoking and having many children.

CERVICAL CANCER

Like all forms of cancer, cervical cancer is an outbreak of uncontrolled abnormal cell growth. Many women who get cervical cancer don't realize that they have the disease, because it doesn't have a lot of symptoms at first. Advanced cervical cancer can cause bleeding or discharge from the vagina that is not normal. If you have any of these signs, see your doctor. They may be caused by something other than cancer, but the only way to know is to see your doctor. There are several risk factors for cervical cancer, the greatest being a high-risk HPV infection. Other risk factors include cigarette smoking, having used birth control pills for five or more years, and having given birth to three or more children.

Cervical cancer is a dangerous disease. For those at risk, it's important to talk to a doctor or other health care provider if you think there's any chance you've been exposed to HPV.

Cervical cancer is easily detected with a regular Pap test. These tests look for precancers and cell changes on the cervix that can lead to cervical cancer if not properly treated. Another method of diagnosing cervical cancer is through an HPV test, which can identify abnormal cells that may be infected with high-risk types of HPV. Women should begin getting Pap tests at age twenty-one, or within three years of their first sexual experience, whichever comes first. They should get Pap tests each year thereafter as part of a regular gynecological exam.

If your doctor discovers that you have cervical cancer, you should ask to be referred to a gynecologic oncologist—a doctor who has been trained to treat cancers of a woman's reproductive system. The gynecologic oncologist will put together a treatment plan to fight the disease. Depending on the stage of the disease, there are three main treatments for cervical cancer:

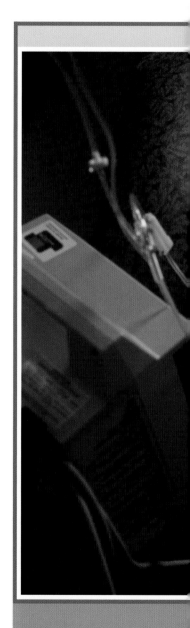

- Surgery. A doctor removes cancerous tissue during an operation.
- Chemotherapy. This treatment uses drugs to stop or slow the growth of cancer cells. Chemotherapy may cause side effects that range from appetite changes and constipation to hair loss and vomiting. But these side effects often get better or go away

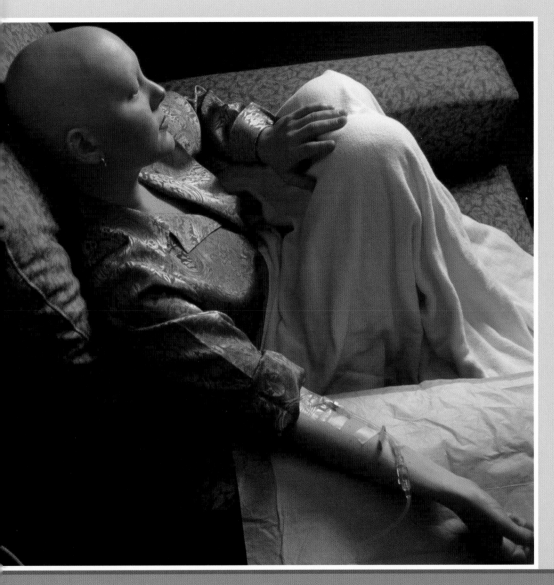

Many people think cancer is a disease that doesn't affect young people. But cervical cancer is common in younger women. Treatments for the disease include chemotherapy, which can cause a person to lose her hair.

altogether once chemotherapy is completed. Chemotherapy drugs may be given in several forms, including pills or through an intravenous injection with a needle.

- Radiation. This method uses high-energy rays (similar to X-rays) to try to kill the cancer cells and stop them from spreading. The rays are aimed at the part of the body where the cancer is.

While there are several treatments for cervical cancer, it is still a deadly disease. That's why preventing the disease is so important. Getting regular Pap tests, always using condoms, limiting your number of sexual partners (or abstaining altogether), and not smoking are great ways to help reduce your cervical cancer risk. And one of the newest, and arguably best, ways of reducing the risk of cervical cancer is getting an HPV vaccination.

Two HPV vaccines, Cervarix and Gardasil, are available to protect girls and women against the types of HPV that cause most cervical, vaginal, and vulvar cancers. Both vaccines are recommended for eleven- and twelve-year-old girls and for those who are thirteen to twenty-six years old who did not get any or all of the shots when they were younger. These vaccines can actually be given to girls as young as nine years of age. Most doctors recommended that females get the same vaccine brand for all three doses whenever possible. It is important to note that even women who are vaccinated against HPV need to have regular Pap tests to screen for cervical cancer, and they should continue to practice safe sex.

CHAPTER three

PREVENTING HPV AND CANCER WITH THE HPV VACCINE

One thing that sets cervical cancer apart from many other types of cancer is that, in many cases, it can be prevented. Since so many cases of cervical cancer are caused by HPV, preventing the disease means cervical cancer can be prevented, too. Abstinence from sex is obviously the best way to prevent this disease. For young women who are sexually active, there are other ways to prevent the disease, including the HPV vaccine.

PREVENTING HPV

Since the connection between HPV and cervical cancer is so clear, it makes sense that the best way to lessen the risk of cervical cancer is to prevent HPV. There are several ways to help prevent this often-undiagnosed disease:

- Abstinence. Since HPV is spread through sexual contact, avoiding sex is the only 100 percent foolproof method of preventing HPV infections.

The only foolproof method for preventing HPV infections is abstaining from sexual contact. For women engaging in sexual contact, condoms and the HPV vaccine can help prevent the disease.

- Condoms. Using condoms helps prevent many STIs, such as HPV, by blocking the exchange of bodily fluids. However, condoms are not 100 percent effective in preventing disease. Factors such as condom malfunction and user error can put women at risk for disease and unplanned pregnancy.
- Limiting the number of sexual partners. By limiting the number of sexual encounters, you greatly reduce the risk of contracting HPV. The more people you have sexual contact with, the more chances you have of coming in contact with the disease. By the same token, choosing partners who haven't had a large number of partners helps reduce your risk of coming in contact with the disease.

While safe sex practices are a good method of preventing HPV infections, the HPV vaccine is one of the newest ways of preventing the disease. There are two vaccines available—Cervarix (made by GlaxoSmithKline) and Gardasil (made by Merck). Work began during the 1980s

23

to develop the vaccine. Over the years, researchers at Georgetown University Medical Center in Washington, D.C., the University of Rochester in Rochester, New York, the University of Queensland in Brisbane, Australia, and the NCI worked simultaneously to develop the vaccine. In 2006, the U.S. Food and Drug Administration (FDA) approved the first HPV vaccine, Gardasil. In 2007, Cervarix was introduced and approved for use in Australia and Europe. It was licensed for use in the United States in 2009.

Both of the HPV vaccines are licensed by the FDA and recommended by the CDC. The vaccines make your body's immune system produce antibodies to certain HPV types. These antibodies protect you from getting infected with HPV. The two share several other similarities:

- Both vaccines are effective against HPV types 16 and 18, which cause most cervical cancers. Both work well to prevent cervical cancer and precancerous cells in women.
- Both are made with very small parts of the human papillomavirus. The parts used in the vaccine are not alive, so neither of the vaccines can cause HPV infection or cancer.
- The vaccines are given as shots and require three doses.
- Both vaccines have been proved safe in several large clinical trials.
- A health care provider must administer them—there are no over-the-counter HPV vaccines.

While the two vaccines have many similarities, they have a few differences as well. The vaccines have different adjuvants, which are substances in the vaccine that increase the body's immune response. The vaccines also differ in that Gardasil is the only one that also protects against HPV types 6 and 11. These HPV types cause most genital warts in females and males.

The vaccines have very few side effects. Possible side effects include bruising, itching, redness, swelling, or tenderness around the area where the shot is given. Women may also experience dizziness, fainting, mild fever, nausea, and vomiting. Such symptoms usually do not last long and generally go away on their own. Not every woman who receives the vaccine experiences side effects. Many do not.

In some women, the HPV vaccine can cause negative side effects. Side effects can range from bruising and itching at the site of the shot to dizziness and mild nausea.

As is the case with any vaccine, there is a very small risk of an allergic reaction. If you get the vaccine and then experience an accelerated heartbeat, high fever, hives, rash, or weakness, call your health care provider right away. If you have difficulty breathing, call 911 immediately.

WHO SHOULD GET THE HPV VACCINE

While anyone can get HPV, the vaccine is only recommended for certain groups. Cervarix and Gardasil are usually given only to girls and women between the ages of nine and twenty-six. According to CDC recommendations, all girls who are eleven or twelve years old should get three doses of either brand of HPV vaccine. The CDC also recommends that if a female between the ages of thirteen and twenty-six has not gotten all three doses of HPV vaccine, she should do so as soon as possible. Because Gardasil also protects against some HPV types that cause genital warts, the CDC recommends that males from age nine to twenty-six also receive this vaccine. HPV vaccination has been shown to reduce HPV infection in males and may decrease risk of certain cancers, such as cancer of the penis or anus.

One of the main reasons for giving the vaccine at such an early age is to make sure

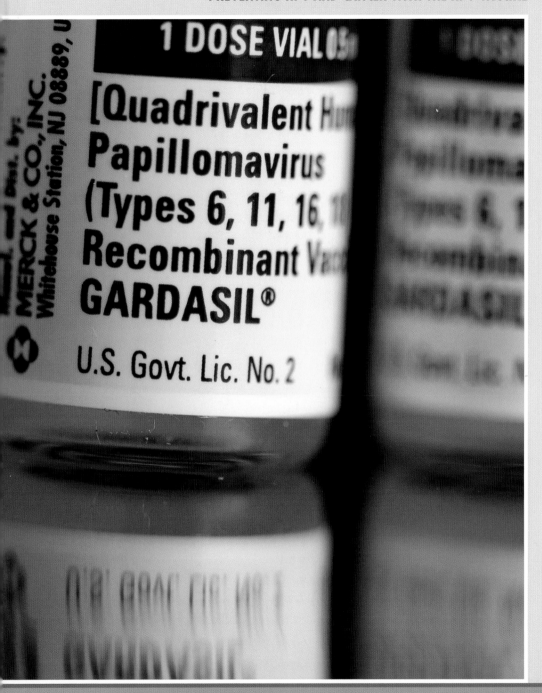

The HPV vaccine comes in two brand choices—Gardasil and Cervarix. Both are administered in three doses by shots. Women must get all three shots for the vaccine to be effective.

that women are vaccinated before they become sexually active and before they could potentially be exposed to HPV. Another good reason for administering the vaccine at this time is that it coincides with the recommended exam given to preteen girls. It is important for girls to get this exam because it gives them a chance to learn about all the changes in their bodies, as well as ask questions and learn how to be safe as they mature and eventually become sexually active.

When you get the vaccine, you will get the second shot two months after the first shot. You will get the third shot four months after the second shot. So, in all, it takes six months to get all three shots. Both Gardasil and Cervarix will protect you against HPV for at least five years. It may last much longer, or you may need a booster shot. More studies need to be done to show how long it lasts.

People who have already had sexual contact before getting all three doses of an HPV vaccine might still benefit if they were not infected before vaccination with the HPV types included in the vaccine they received. The best way to be sure that a person gets the most benefit from HPV vaccination is to complete all three doses before sexual activity begins. Women and men should also be sure to get all three doses, as just getting one or two doses does not ensure that you will be protected against the diseases.

Pregnant women are not advised to get the HPV vaccine. If they want to be vaccinated, they should wait until after they give birth to get the vaccine. If a woman does get the vaccine while pregnant, she should hold off on getting any more doses until giving birth. She should also notify her doctor immediately, just in case there are any side effects.

If you already have an HPV infection, the HPV vaccine will not treat it. The vaccine is only able to prevent new infections, and it does not cure the disease. However, there are treatments available for genital warts and for cell changes that may lead to cervical cancer. If you think that you may have HPV, talk with your health care provider about what tests and treatments you may need.

Even if you get the HPV vaccine, there is still a small risk that you can get an HPV infection that causes genital warts or leads to cervical cancer. The HPV vaccine does not protect against all types of HPV that can cause cancer. That means it is still important for you to get regular Pap tests each year to detect any cell changes that can lead to cervical cancer.

The decision to get the HPV vaccine is a very important one. It is something that you should discuss with your parents or other trusted adults.

GETTING THE VACCINE

Once you make the decision to get the HPV vaccine, you need to choose where to obtain it. You can get the vaccine from your doctor or health care provider. You can also get the vaccine from Planned Parenthood clinics, your local health department, or family planning centers. Your doctor or health care provider can explain how the vaccine works, outline the possible risks, and answer any questions you may have about the disease and the vaccine. It is very important to ask all the questions you have about HPV, the vaccine, and your reproductive health in general. Although these may be embarrassing questions to ask, or you may be afraid to ask with your parent present, it is essential to get all the information you can when you get the vaccine.

Like many medications, the HPV vaccine is relatively expensive. Each shot costs roughly $125, making a full dosage of the vaccine (three shots) $375. Many health insurance companies will cover all or most of the cost of the vaccine. If you do not have health insurance, or if your insurance plan does not cover the vaccine, there are other ways to get assistance in paying for the vaccine.

One way of getting help to pay for vaccines is the Vaccines for Children (VFC) program. This government program helps families of eligible children in the United States who might not otherwise have access to vaccines. The program provides vaccines at no cost to doctors who

Women can get the HPV vaccine from doctors and clinics such as Planned Parenthood. Planned Parenthood is also a good source for information about HPV and the HPV vaccine.

serve eligible children. Children younger than nineteen years of age are able to receive VFC vaccines if they are Medicaid-eligible, American Indian, Alaskan Native, or have no health insurance. Children who have health insurance that does not cover the vaccination can receive

VFC vaccines through federally qualified health centers or rural health centers. Parents of children who receive vaccines through the VFC program should check with their health care providers about possible administrative fees that might apply. These fees help providers cover the costs for services like storing the vaccines and paying staff members to give vaccines to patients.

If you are not sure how to pay for the HPV vaccine, it is a good idea to talk to your doctor or health care provider about payment options. He or she may be able to give you information about programs that can help you with the fees associated with the vaccine.

MYTHS
AND
FACTS

MYTH   **If a person doesn't have genital warts, he or she can't give me HPV.**

FACT   Most people with HPV don't exhibit any symptoms. Most high-risk strains of HPV associated with cervical cancer do not produce genital warts. So even if a person doesn't have visible symptoms, he or she can still have, and pass on, HPV to you.

MYTH   **Young women can't get cervical cancer.**

FACT   Although cervical cancer can occur at any age, women as young as twenty have gotten cervical cancer. Because young women can be infected with HPV and not know it, their risk of developing the disease when they get older is much greater.

MYTH   **If I get the HPV vaccine, I won't need to use condoms.**

FACT   If you are sexually active, you should always use condoms. Even though the HPV vaccine protects you against HPV infection and decreases the risk of cervical cancer, it does not protect against other STIs or pregnancy. So it is very important to use protection every single time you have sex.

CHAPTER **four**

THE VACCINE: CONTROVERSY AND AWARENESS

As with most reproductive health issues, the vaccine for the HPV virus has garnered its share of controversy. Many people are excited about the vaccine and its ability to help prevent not only HPV, but also cervical cancer. Others have questioned the use of the vaccine because it seems geared mostly toward young women and girls. They have concerns that the vaccine may encourage young women to become sexually active. Even if you are unsure where you stand on the issue, or if you have a firm opinion either for or against the vaccine, it is important to consider both sides of the argument.

SUPPORT FOR THE VACCINE

Since cervical cancer is such a deadly disease, the introduction of a vaccine that could possibly prevent it was big news. Many people were very excited about and supportive of the vaccine, as it has the potential to save lives. Some of the biggest proponents of the vaccine are doctors and other members of the health care

The Centers for Disease Control (CDC) has endorsed use of the HPV vaccine as an effective method for preventing HPV infections and reducing the risk of cervical cancer.

community, especially those who regularly treat women. They realize the importance of preventing HPV as a method of reducing the occurrence of cervical cancer. They also know that the vaccine is safe and doesn't have any serious side effects, so it is safe for most people to use.

Cancer research groups and other disease research groups, such as the NCI and the CDC, have all advocated for the use of the HPV vaccine. Because of the link between HPV and cervical cancer, these groups see a highly effective way to prevent cervical cancer, something that is nearly impossible with most other cancers. Women's health groups, such as Planned Parenthood, are also strong advocates of the vaccine. Since they are interested in improving both reproductive health and the health of women in general, the vaccine falls right in line with their mission.

Another proponent of the vaccine has been state legislatures. In the first few years after Gardasil was approved, several state legislatures introduced bills that would make it mandatory for young women to be vaccinated before they begin school. Michigan was the first state to introduce one of these bills, but it was not enacted. Only two such bills were passed—in Virginia and Washington, D.C.

Legislators in at least forty-one states and Washington, D.C., have introduced legislation to require, fund, or educate the public about the HPV vaccine. At least nineteen states have enacted this legislation—Colorado, Indiana, Iowa, Louisiana, Maine, Maryland, Michigan, Minnesota, Nevada, New Mexico, New York, North Carolina, North Dakota, Rhode Island, South Dakota, Texas, Utah, Virginia, and Washington. The CDC announced that the New Hampshire health department announced in 2006 that it would provide the vaccine at no cost to girls under age eighteen. Since then, the department has distributed thousands of doses of the vaccine to girls in the state. South Dakota's governor also announced a similar plan in January 2007 that combines $7.5 million in federal vaccine funds and $1.7 million from the state's general fund. As a result, thousands of young women in South Dakota have received the vaccine as well. The Washington state legislature approved spending $10 million to voluntarily vaccinate ninety-four thousand girls over a span of two years.

In Texas, the governor issued an executive order that required girls to be vaccinated before they enter the sixth grade. However, the Texas legislature overrode the order and barred mandatory vaccination in the state until at least 2011. Most of the states that have enacted laws requiring the vaccine also have opt-out policies. This means if a girl cannot afford the vaccine, or if her parents do not want her to have it, she can decline getting vaccinated.

OPPOSITION TO THE VACCINE

Once the HPV vaccine was introduced, many felt it should be added to the mandatory vaccines that children receive while they are in school (vaccinations such as those for measles, mumps, and rubella). However, the suggestion of making the vaccine mandatory has received a lot of opposition from several groups.

Much of the opposition to the vaccine comes from conservative and religious groups. Several of these organizations, such as Focus on the Family and the Family Research Council, support widespread availability of the HPV vaccine, but they are very opposed to mandatory vaccinations for young women. They feel that making the vaccine mandatory lessens parental rights, forcing parents to allow their children to be vaccinated whether they want them to be or not. Many of these groups also oppose the vaccine's use because they believe it encourages young women to be sexually active and/or promiscuous (having sex with

Some states have made the HPV vaccine a required vaccination for female students. Other groups oppose this, and the use of the vaccine in general, as they worry it encourages teens to be sexually active.

many different partners). These groups often encourage abstinence-only sex education, so they are opposed to giving young people birth control, condoms, and other forms of STI protection.

For some of these same reasons, many parents are opposed to having their teen and preteen daughters vaccinated against HPV. They do not want to think about the possibility of their daughters getting a sexually transmitted infection, and they often do not think that their child is at risk of contracting HPV. Some parents are also fearful that if they allow their child to be vaccinated against an STI, they will become more sexually active or less careful during sexual contact. Parents are also sometimes fearful that giving their child the vaccine will make them think that they are completely protected against the virus. This could be problematic for a young woman, because the vaccine does not protect against every single type of HPV or against other STIs, so they still need to be careful and use other forms of protection during sexual contact.

Other groups that are opposed to mandatory HPV vaccinations for young women are many health insurance companies. These companies do not want to be required to pay for the vaccination, which is quite expensive. They also do not want the number of women receiving the vaccine to increase dramatically, which it would if it was required, because it would tax these companies' resources due to dramatically increased payouts for the vaccine.

THE FUTURE OF THE HPV VACCINE

While the HPV vaccines that are available now do a great deal to prevent the disease, there are still strains they do not affect. Because of that, researchers are continually working to create new versions of the vaccine to provide broader protection against the disease. With further research, drug companies hope to be able to produce vaccines that protect women against all strains of

Researchers are continually working on the HPV vaccine to make it more effective. Preventing cervical cancer is an important job, and the role of the HPV vaccine in that is essential.

HPV, ensuring 100 percent protection against the disease and, thus, cervical cancer.

As researchers work to create improved versions of the vaccine, legislators and nonprofit organizations work to make the vaccine more accessible to more people. They hope to make the vaccine more afford-able, which will make it available to a wider audience. Because cervical cancer is so dangerous and HPV is so common, it is very important for as many women to be protected from the disease as possible. And because the vaccine is so effective, it is essential to make it available to every young woman who wants to get it.

abstinence The practice of refraining from sexual activity for medical, psychological, social, or religious reasons.

adjuvant A substance that enhances the body's immune system response to an antigen, a foreign substance.

antibody A protein that circulates in the blood and is produced in response to a specific antigen. Antibodies combine chemically with substances that the body recognizes as alien, such as bacteria and viruses.

cervical cancer A dangerous type of cancer that affects the cervix.

cervix The narrow necklike passage forming the lower end of the uterus.

chemotherapy The treatment of disease, most commonly cancer, through the use of chemical substances.

controversy A dispute or discussion between two sides of an issue.

genital wart A small growth in the anal or genital area caused by a virus that is usually spread by sexual contact.

gynecologic oncologist A doctor who specializes in the diagnosis and treatment of women with cancer of the reproductive organs.

human papillomavirus (HPV) A sexually transmitted virus that can cause genital warts and cervical cancer. There are over one hundred types of HPV.

mandatory Containing or comprising a command.

nonprofit An organization that does not distribute surplus wealth to owners or shareholders, but instead uses the extra funds to meet its goals.

outbreak A sudden increase in the symptoms of a disease, particularly a sexually transmitted infection (STI).

Pap test A screening test used in gynecology to detect cancerous cells in the cervix; also called a Pap smear, cervical smear, or smear test.

precancerous In the state of having the ability to lead to cancer if left untreated.

promiscuous Having sexual contact with many different partners.

proponent An individual or group that is supportive of a theory or cause.

radiation The treatment of cancer using X-rays or similar forms of radiation.

sexually transmitted infection (STI) An infection that a person can get from having sex with someone who has the infection.

strain A type or variety of a disease.

symptom The evidence of a disease or physical disturbance.

transmission The passing of a communicable disease from an infected party to someone who is not infected.

vaccine A substance used to stimulate the production of antibodies and provide immunity against one or several diseases.

FOR MORE INFORMATION

American Cancer Society
250 Williams Street, NW
Atlanta, GA 30303
(800) 227-2345
Web site: http://www.cancer.org
The mission of the American Cancer Society is to eliminate cancer as
    a major health problem.

Canadian Cancer Society Research Institute
10 Alcorn Avenue, Suite 200
Toronto, ON M4V 3B1
Canada
(416) 961-7223
Web site: http://www.cancer.ca
The Canadian Cancer Society Research Institute works through
    research to help treat and prevent cancer.

Canadian Federation for Sexual Health
1 Nicholas Street, Suite 430
Ottawa, ON K1N 7B7
Canada
(613) 241-4474
Web site: http://www.cfsh.ca
The Canadian Federation for Sexual Health has member organizations
    in communities across Canada providing clinical services, education,
    and counseling to hundreds of thousands of Canadians every year.

Centers for Disease Control and Prevention
1600 Clifton Road

Atlanta, GA 30333
(800) 232-4636
Web site: http://www.cdc.gov
The Centers for Disease Control and Prevention is one of the major
operating components of the Department of Health and Human
Services.

Gilda's Club Worldwide
48 Wall Street, 11th Floor
New York, NY 10005
(888) GILDA-4-U
Web site: http://www.gildasclub.org
Email: info@gildasclub.org
Gilda's Club is an organization dedicated to creating support for
cancer patients, their families, and friends.

National Cancer Institute
6116 Executive Boulevard, Suite 300
Bethesda, MD 20892-8322
(800) 422-6237
Web site: http://www.cancer.gov
The National Cancer Institute is part of the National Institutes of
Health, which is one of eleven agencies that compose the
Department of Health and Human Services. It is the federal
government's principal agency for cancer research and training.

Planned Parenthood Federation of America
434 West 33rd Street

New York, NY 10001
(212) 541-7800
Web site: http://www.plannedparenthood.org
Planned Parenthood is a health care provider and advocate for
  women's health issues.

WEB SITES

Due to the changing nature of Internet links, Rosen Publishing has
developed an online list of Web sites related to the subject of this book.
This site is updated regularly. Please use this link to access the list:

http://www.rosenlinks.com/gh/hpv

FOR FURTHER READING

Corinna, Heather. *S.E.X.: The All-You-Need-to-Know Progressive Sexuality Guide to Get You Through High School and College.* Cambridge, MA: DaCapo Press, 2007.

Dizon, Don S., and Michael L. Krychman. *Questions & Answers About Human Papilloma Virus* (HPV) (100 Questions & Answers About). Sudbury, MA: Jones and Bartlett Publishers, 2010.

Egendorf, Laura K. *STDs* (At Issue Series). Farmington Hills, MI: Greenhaven Press, 2007.

Hirschman, Kris. *Cervical Cancer* (Diseases and Disorders). Farmington Hills, MI: Lucent Books, 2010.

Holmes, Melissa, and Trish Hutchison. *Hang-Ups, Hook-Ups, and Holding Out: Stuff You Need to Know About Your Body, Sex, and Dating* (Girlology). Deerfield Beach, FL: HCI, 2007.

Hyde, Margaret O. *Safe Sex 101: An Overview for Teens.* Minneapolis, MN: Lerner, 2006.

Krishnan, Shobha. *The HPV Vaccine Controversy: Sex, Cancer, God, and Politics: A Guide for Parents, Women, Men, and Teenagers.* Santa Barbara, CA: Praeger, 2008.

Madison, Amber. *Hooking Up: A Girl's All-Out Guide to Sex and Sexuality.* Amherst, NY: Prometheus Books, 2006.

Spencer, Juliet. *Cervical Cancer* (Deadly Diseases and Epidemics). New York, NY: Chelsea House Publications, 2007.

Westheimer, Ruth, and Pierre A. Lehu. *Dr. Ruth's Guide to Teens and Sex Today: From Social Networking to Friends with Benefits.* New York, NY: Teachers College Press, 2008.

INDEX

ABOUT THE AUTHOR

Jennifer Bringle is a writer and editor who lives in Greensboro, North Carolina. She has written several books for young adults.

PHOTO CREDITS